Saint David's Day

Saint David's Day

Poems by
FLORENCE BULL

Allison & Busby, London

First published in 1972 by
Allison & Busby Limited
6a Noel Street, London W1V 3RB

SBN 85031 074 1

PRINTED IN GREAT BRITAIN BY
THE BOWERING PRESS, PLYMOUTH
AND BOUND BY
G. & J. KITCAT LTD, LONDON

Acknowledgements

The author acknowledges with gratitude an award of £500 made in 1971 by the Society of Authors, trustees of the Eric Gregory Memorial Fund.

'The Well-born' was first published in *Poverty*, the journal of the Child Poverty Action Group.

Contents

I thought, if I could draw my paines,
Through Rimes vexation, I should them allay.

JOHN DONNE

War Poet

Through twenty aeroplaning years
I learned to face the awful blank
somewhere behind which so excited
two loved strangers once, they
spawned me. I held the magic glass
of history which showed a vale of screams
where flesh was torn and rotted and grew dry
on fields of farmers speaking other tongues than mine.

Now you walk out from that same blank,
sound, wholesome, whole and warm, you
sorrowfully sing the horror, mercifully
sing the wasted boys. Alas, alas,
there is no blood on me, my wounds
are too concealed to move you to my need.

Sonnet in six lines

Manic swooping cobs of brown defiance,
sparrows, dance an aerial mass
with all the twittering buildingness
of Spring, but in the looking-glass
I see a magpie couple, childless,
indicting me with their obscene alliance.

The Well-born

'Penny for the guy!'
They halt the aesthete at the Faculty gate,
and his discerning eye approves
the smooth caramel of wet faces
tilting upwards in the sodium glare.
Their effigy lies slumped against the wall.
Finding a copper coin, he burrows
in his Crombie for something to add to it,
smiles a benediction, and moving off
he hears, 'Don't you go buying crisps with that,
Eugene'.

to Joan's baby

hello (whose
small warm
mother wandered
wondered wept
laughed was
bewildered with
me then
suddenly smiled
and made
you) little
living act
of glorious
affirmation.

Darren

a lively cork that
bobs along the garden wall,
sees diamonds in the dirt
and heaps them in the gutter
with starfish hands (whose
smile each time we meet
dissolves the buildings)
today is going to school
to learn the words of meanings.

mister capital i

meet mister capital i,
the capital man who
wrote the capital thesis
teaches capital chemistry
and won several capital
prizes on the way to
the capital top (upon
reaching which his lower
case Wife, he found,
had lower case Left him).

spring song

these fluttering flakes of brown,
these most determined objects
who defile my doorstep every
april day, are teaching me
a truth I might have missed
for all our complicated arabesques
of longing. the trees are bare
this late, the wind is harsh,
and i, unfeeling giant,
stand guard to rid the porch
of air-borne nuisances. yet
love will not be ruled by
unpropitious circumstance:
defying fear and reason they
will build their nests against
the coming certainty of summer
and black flies.

thisshortfatuglydogwith
the
long
face
GIVESMEASHOCK
by showing me before I even ask its
ey es
v r l w n w t l v
o e f o i g i h o e
I
st
oop
to say
thank you
to my joyous friend, whose
owner KICKS it
where-
upon,
of course, I w a l k a w a y

nobody known, so
sweetly poised
on the brink of a
wanted is
whose? clutch lunge miss squash
and then
resent
coldly throbs waswards
through realms of said

sausage fingers

Cherry Tree in Autumn

Wearing my own true colours,
kinder by far than spring's
most adolescent blossoms,
Tree you goldenly are full
of sudden will to soothe.
No fierce demanding promises
frightening to the fragments
of my summer-shattered self.
Stay gold a little while until
I gather strength to face
the helpless blackness of
your poor bare branches
in the glare of winter's
naughty sky.

Christmas 1970

We have at last assented to the wheel
And bound ourselves grimacing to its rim:
Though guns are quieted to honour Him
Who this tradition tells will heal
Our natural wounds, there still
Persists the building of technologies
To debrisfy all hopes, philosophies,
And in one wilful holocaust, the will.

I can give you

Garlands of golden leaves,
And a promise of snow;
A winter with no spring;
Chains of delicate words
To bind you although
You can shred all I bring
With one sharp syllable.

With one sharp syllable
You stopped the song that I was wont to sing,
More lastingly than I would have you know.
When I displayed for you my tentative verbs,
You chose renounce, in dread of helpless cling.
My life has fled you since you served it so,
And will not sing to you of how it grieves.

Saint David's Day

The sweet and wilful daffodil defies
the snows of March and catches laughing
at my heart's eye as it wanders
dismally this day in which the seasons
are compounded. The year's first late
confusing whiteness cannot confound
this greenest blade of purpose, spearing
the wet October leaves, still lying.

Soon the drop will open to reveal,
dispelling all resistance, its triumphal
yellow standard, symbol of
the land that gave me you,
my sweet and wilful heartful,
son of Wales.

*

All week I have been without you,
watching the garden where the roses
still flaunt their colours,
but the scent has gone.

The eggs have hatched in the nest I showed you,
where each mating moment complemented what we did.
Just now the father bird confronted me
with three worms in his beak,
one flickering.

The blossom I picked was fragile.
It had dirty leaves.

Seeing you by the river with your children,
I recollected how our limbs have wound in passion,
but could not recall the taste of your hair.

when you have been away,
i lose my sense of frailty
& greet your coming back
with words that bruise
themselves in stumbling.
until you calm and stop me with
your long white movements,
then i sleep.
and then i wake
& even if your hair is full
of trains my recreated eyes
can recognise in your eyes
watching me, the truth
of our gay sacrament.

Holiday

Alien in this land where wobbling infants
lisp the tongue that you are heir to,
I set out each bright evening to catalogue
the place's facts, seeking in rocks and waves
the clues I fail to find in castled stone and
worded paper, of your carried past.

It is a loving country, of big tombs
and little horses, and owls impatient
for the tardy dark, whose petulance
is quieter than the gulls' the boys disturb
where chapels stand unblinking sentinels
over the frilly fringes of the sea.

But this is all less eloquent of Wales, than
in my English city, your red exiled head.

i am defined now as a function
of your acts. when unexpectedly
we meet i am the whispering leaf
that trembles on the breeze of your
hello. in your smile's warmth i am
the land that wakes at sunrise, your
laughter makes me fields of flowers.
at night and morning i am the seashore
yearning to your tides, between whose
coming in and going out i am the lute
whose strings were never plucked to
any sweetness until by your hands.
and if you go away i am the small
wet friendless mouse who snivels
in the cornfield's stubble underneath
the rain that will not stop.

Self-sacrifice

What little I have learned of gardening,
mostly from old ladies here and there,
has come in usefully in this:
Pruning was what they taught me,
and more especially, to recognise
the stifling sucker by its seven leaves.
So calm and competent, I grasp
the menace I have named to you
as love, ignoring thorns
since by the act I nourish growth
in more legitimate directions.
And all the time my own reality
is watching impotent,
a frantic greenfly in a disinfected bottle.

Now

the cycle ends,
as life does,
in consultations
and in whispering.
then panic then
despair and then
the permanence
of knowing
what we
shared
was very
little
after
all,
com-
pared
with
this

reality.

Poem without a title

mochyn

(you asked me to a funeral &
I went mourning for the corpse I)

cariad

Your name

One syllable round and
weighty, like a cat's
bulk landing surely on
those four deft, tiny paws,
and then the second settling
after it like fur round flesh.
That's how they call you
in your country's tongue.

And though I have peopled my
new world with keener names,
daft and unmalicious, yours gets
in my way, like a soft old
comfortable cat I have to stoop
and move, almost without noticing.

dearly beloved,

i am writing this from my new room,
i am not telling you the address, because
i do not want to see you again.

my new room is long and narrow, with
a hole in the wall, and
for several days i waited
for a tiny mouse-face to appear, but none did.

as i write, a moth is circling the light bulb
at the other end of the room,
soon it will die and i shall be alone.

with all my love,

The Death of the Long-Lived Lie

Neurotic with No,
I paraded all my best resentments,
The old hurt unavenged,
The malice he had fathered on me.

Watching his eyes, I heard my voice
Grow colder till he rose to go.
And then I said goodbye and dared
My life to let him touch me.

(and sobbing Yes broke into me,
spread out, and burgled all my nerves)

Look, Snow
has done to the city
what you do to me.
By laying (oh!)
white fingers on her
he has brought out
all her beauties,
so that buildings
we had thought
flat-fronted
now excite us
as we feel them
with our eyes.

Lovely War

When they did up the local,
they called it "The Lovely War",
with flags and a few coronation mugs,
the odd sepia group, and badges.
I sat in there with Arthur,
him wheezing from the gas of
fifty years ago, and poured his beer
into the only glass his hands can hold.
At seventy-five he has less time
than I have for complaining, busy
with the job that supplements
the pensions that they gave him: one for
the boy who was an officer, one for
the father who survived his sons.

Teacher

Childless at thirty, I indulge
in hardness or in fantasies.
A private pupil is "my little boy"
who comes to solemnly attend
a grammar lesson, and bites
his lip at what I say to him,
and battles to the end with
nouns and verbs, until triumphant,
putting on his coat, he bursts out
that he's playing for the fourth year team.
I struggle too, with life's bewildering
syntax, and with the urge to talk about
my class in bed, a habit which
I learn can lose me love.

When Spring's First Lilacs shock your nose,
do you bewail their fading in advance?
detect within the radiance of the rose,
its falling? hear the rattling dance
of death in every infant's cry?
Do you see winter's snow in summer's sky?
(and when I kiss you, are you quite aware
that we are moving gravewards? Do you care?)

Then why (Reluctant Lover) do you grieve
our final parting from the very start?
and formulate such sadness as to leave
no room for gladness in your heart?

Before you can do penance for your sin,
you must commit it. Come, let us begin!

Unconfident, uncertain of your art,
you manipulate so carefully my
fractured sense of happiness, assuring
me that if I fall again I will not
break it. You mind my hesitation though
you do not show it, hiding your sorrow
each time I fail to answer your advance.
So I am punished only by the fear
that you will weary of my clumsiness
before I am persuaded by the rhythm
of your movements, and suddenly recall
how long ago I used to love to dance.

The Female Father

Where is the language to supply a name
for my unnatural parenthood?
Where is the art to frame hosannas
for my daughter, whom another womb has borne?
Where is the skill to guide this life
away from the uncertainty of its emergence?
Where shall we look to find the hope,
the courage and the wisdom? (And the shame?)

Children ourselves in this hard mystery,
Love is all we can look to,
Love that has made a female father of me,
by blessing with a Springtime blossoming
the life of him whose is the only
life I have.

The North of Two Countries

Squeezed through the distances of an afternoon,
in the train that smells dirtier than the
orange dust caking its windows looks,
I cannot avoid the faded cabbage tints
of winter hillsides, scored by dun cuttings
of the rails no longer vigorous, shamefaced.

Soon the scarred contours will be forsaken
by this poor miracle, leaving the grey road
then to furnish my journeyings, fainthearted
and discouraged as the dim canal. My torn
imagination travels livelier, westward:
Wales, your distances are calling me again.